spiritual paths

forgiveness

spiritual paths

forgiveness

jay vickers

contents

introduction forgiveness in our lives

What is forgiveness?

According to the dictionaries, forgiveness means remitting a debt or pardoning an offense or an offender.

But it's a lot more than that, and much more complicated. Asking for or granting forgiveness can be one of the most difficult things to do—and one of the simplest.

For Christians, Jews, Muslims, and members of other religions, the word "**forgiveness**" is most closely associated with God. God is perfect—we are not. We do things that are wrong, that offend God, that fall short of the standard that God wants from us. If we ever want to be "**at one**" with God, we have to ask for God's forgiveness. Later in this book, we'll see what the scriptures of various religions say about God's forgiveness.

But forgiveness between people is just as important. The Christian Lord's Prayer asks God to "forgive us our trespasses, as we forgive those who trespass against us." If we are not prepared to forgive other people, why should we expect God to forgive us?

And what about forgiving ourselves? This is something that is often forgotten, but our ability to forgive others or to ask for their forgiveness depends on our being able to show clemency to ourselves.

Although this book won't tell you everything there is to know about forgiveness, it will provide some inspirational thoughts and challenging ideas on the subject. Each chapter deals with a separate aspect of forgiveness.

We begin with forgiveness and other people: your family, your friends, and also those with whom you might not get along. **Next**, we look at a specific problem area: forgiveness within intimate relationships, such as marriage. Many partnerships break up because one person won't forgive the other, whether for something as minor as a harsh word or as major as adultery. We will look at how to overcome problems in your relationship and how to prevent new ones from arising. **Then**, we explore how you can forgive, heal, and be at peace with yourself—often the most difficult of all people to forgive.

The focus then shifts to your relationship with God, and the concept of sin—the reason why we need God's forgiveness, whatever God is to you.

First, we look at how sin harms yourself and others, and separates you from God. Next, we consider the joy and peace that God's forgiveness brings. Finally, we look at how to make it right, both with God and with other people. Forgiveness isn't just saying sorry and being pardoned. It's about changing your life, and the lives of those around you, for the better.

The last chapter brings all of these ideas together within the context of the difficulties of forgiveness. Why can it be so hard to give forgiveness, or to accept it, whether in your relationship with God, with other people, or with yourself? Are there some things that are unforgivable? What role does understanding play in the arena of forgiveness?

This book is designed to be read in different ways—straight through from beginning to end, one chapter at a time, or by dipping in at any point. Sometimes an idea might be spread over several pages, and you may need to turn back a few pages to follow the train of thought from its beginning.

Most of the quotations stand on their own, so you can open the book at random and find a source of spiritual inspiration or comfort. But many of them also illustrate or expand on specific ideas in the text. So if you find a quotation you particularly like, or that seems especially helpful to you, you might want to read the pages before and after it to see how it fits in.

Most of all, this book has been written to inspire you, to help you understand the nature of forgiveness, the need for forgiveness, and to guide you in making things right with God, with other people, and with yourself.

Dear Lord and Father of mankind
Forgive our foolish ways
Reclothe us in our rightful mind
In purer lives thy service find
In deeper reverence praise

J. G. Whittier (1807–1892)

We need forgiveness because we are foolish, or thoughtless, or careless. Because we are selfish and greedy. Because we lie to protect ourselves at the expense of others. Because we sometimes deliberately set out to hurt others. Because we use harsh words to wound. Because we take what isn't ours. The list is endless. . . . **We need forgiveness.**

J. G. Whittier's hymn on page 19 makes the point that forgiveness isn't the end of the process, but only the beginning.

After we have been forgiven, we need to move on, to lead "purer lives," to help others, and to worship and serve God.

Grant, we beseech thee, merciful Lord, to thy faithful people pardon and peace, that they may be cleansed from all their sins, and serve thee with a quiet mind.

Book of Common Prayer

In our relationship with God, we should always be aware that even our best is not good enough. If we approach God in humility, and acknowledge our unworthiness, we will be granted forgiveness and the joy of God's presence.

But, independently of my own works and warfare,
Independently of my faith or unfaith, good or evil,
Independently of my poor devotion to Thee,
And of my thoughts and the thoughts of hundreds
like me,
I fix my hopes on Thy mercy alone.

Whether Thou adjudge me upright or rebellious,
I sue for free pardon from Thy unbought justice.
O Lord, who art gracious without thought of
consequence,
I set my face toward that free grace of Thine.

The Masnavi Book 5, Rumi (1207–1273
(Sufi writings

Sometimes in our arrogance we may believe that we don't actually need forgiveness. "After all, I'm not that bad a person, am I?"
Think again.

According to the Bible:

For all have sinned, and come short of the glory of God.

Romans 3:23

There is no room for doubt here.

In the Christian tradition, to think that we don't need forgiveness is perhaps the greatest sin of all:

Pride.

Other belief systems, too, warn against presuming that we don't need God's forgiveness.

Beware lest the fire of thy presumptuousness debar thee from attaining to God's Holy Court. Turn unto Him, and fear not because of thy deeds. He, in truth, forgiveth whomsoever He desireth as a bounty on His part; no God is there but Him, the Ever-Forgiving, the All-Bounteous.

Kitáb-i-Aqdas
(Bahá'í scriptures)

And so we turn to God, confess our faults, and say (and mean!) that we are sorry for them. We resolve not to commit them again, and ask God to forgive us. And God has promised us forgiveness.

But what about our relations with the people we share our lives with? How should forgiveness figure in our daily lives?

Do not call attention to the faults of others, nor boast of your own excellence.

T'ai-Shang Kan-Ying P'ien
(Taoist scriptures)

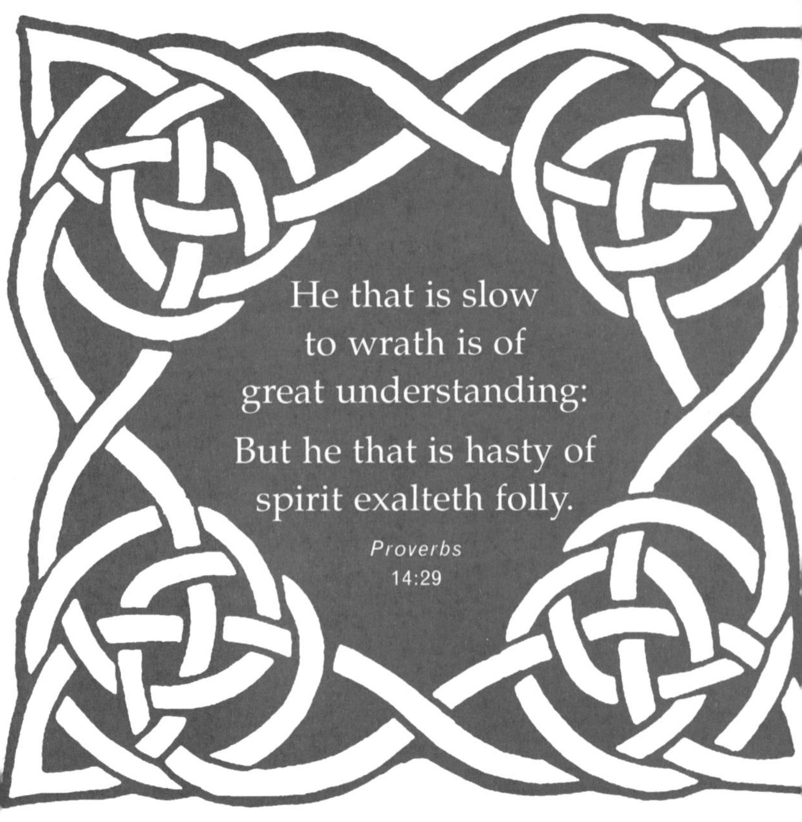
He that is slow
to wrath is of
great understanding:
But he that is hasty of
spirit exalteth folly.
Proverbs
14:29

If we leap on each other's faults, if we are critical of every trivial failing of those we live and work with, then we are creating sins in other people, which then need to be forgiven if there is to be peace.

It is far better to accept other people's everyday faults and failings as part of the inherent weakness of humanity. After all, you're not perfect, so why should you expect others to be?

Your own actions can irritate, annoy, hurt, displease, or anger other people. You have a responsibility for the results of your words and deeds. You have a duty to other people, just as they have to you.

It is impossible but that
offenses will come:
But woe unto him, through
whom they come!

Luke 17:1

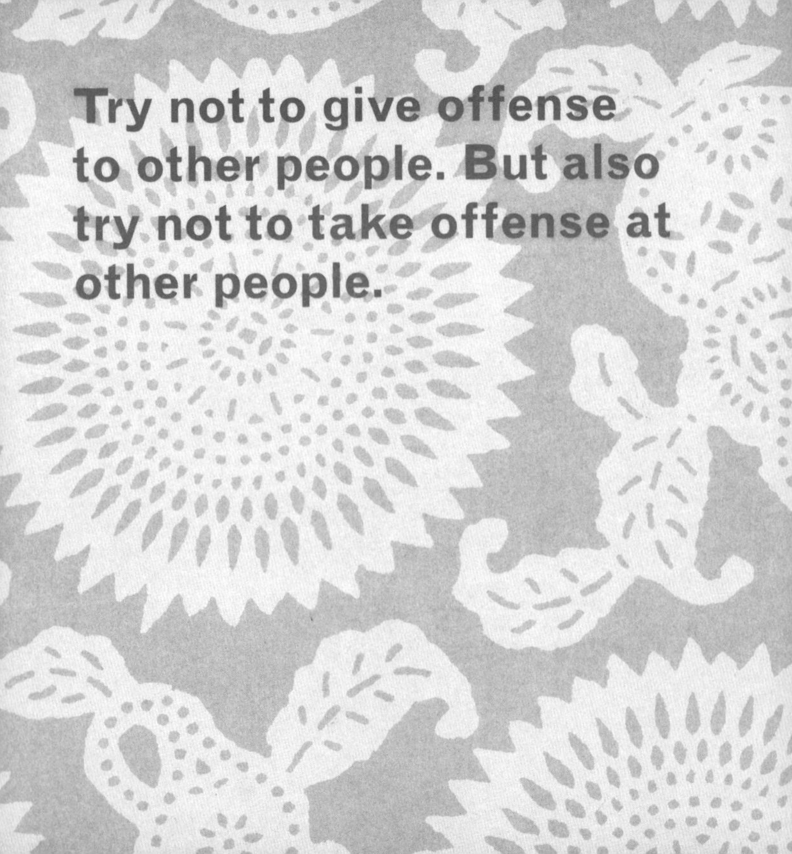

Try not to give offense to other people. But also try not to take offense at other people.

Forbearing one another,
and forgiving one another,
if any man have a quarrel
against any: even as Christ
forgave you, so also do ye.

Colossians 3:13

We look at some people as exemplars, as living saints. These are people we can't imagine doing anything wrong.

But these people, if they are the saints we think they are, will be far more conscious of their own failings than we are, or than we are of our own faults.

Remember that there is a little bit of bad even in the best of us.

And a little bit of good even in the worst of us.

In all aspects, people's lives are a mixture of good and bad. So when we look at other people, we should look first for the good in them—because those who look for evil will always find it.

He redeemed his vices with his virtues. There was ever more in him to be praised than to be pardoned.

Ben Jonson (1573–1637) on Shakespeare (1564–1616)

Judge not, and ye shall not be judged;
Condemn not, and ye shall not be
condemned;
Forgive, and ye shall be forgiven.

Luke 6:37

Our relations with other people should involve forgiveness every day. When we see other people's faults, we should first stop, step back, and enumerate our own.

Only when we have dealt with our own failings do we have the right to turn to those of others.

First rectify thyself and then convert others.

T'ai-Shang Kan-Ying P'ien
(Taoist scriptures)

Why beholdedst thou the mote [speck] that is in thy brother's eye, but considerest not the beam that is in thine own eye?

Or how wilt thou say to thy brother, Let me pull out the mote out of thine eye; and behold, a beam is in thine own eye?

Thou hypocrite, first cast out the beam out of thine own eye; and then shalt thou see clearly to cast out the mote out of thy brother's eye.

Matthew 7:3–5

We can do nothing to earn God's forgiveness, except be honest.

If we are prepared to own up to our sins, God will be prepared to forgive them.

When he thus enumerates his sins and faults,
God at last will grant him pardon as a free gift,
Saying, "O angels, bring him back to me,
Since the eyes of his heart were set on hope,
Without care for consequences I set him free,
And draw the pen through the record of his sins!"

The Masnavi Book 5, Rumi (1207–1273)
(Sufi writings)

There is a great nobility in forgiveness:

To suffer woes which Hope thinks infinite;
To forgive wrongs darker than death or night;
  To defy Power, which seems omnipotent;
To love, and bear; to hope till Hope creates
From its own wreck the thing it contemplates;
  Neither to change, not falter, nor repent;
This, like thy glory, Titan, is to be
Good, great and joyous, beautiful and free;
This is alone Life, Joy, Empire and Victory.

Prometheus Unbound, Percy Bysshe Shelley,
(1792–1822)

forgiveness

with family, friends, and foes

Forgiveness, like charity, should begin at home, with children, with partners, with parents.

We pardon in proportion as we love.

François, Duc de la Rochefoucauld (1613–1680)

For a mother of a young child, forgiveness, like love, is unconditional.

If her four-year-old son knocks over and breaks her favorite vase, she may be upset or angry, she may even shout at him—but she will forgive him, because she is his mother, he is her son. She knows he'll do it again, or something similar; but still she forgives him.

As the child grows older, when he says, "I'm sorry," his mother will say, "Do you really mean that?" before she pardons him.

For forgiveness to be given, there needs to be evidence of contrition.

Contrition doesn't just mean saying sorry, it means saying (and believing), "I won't do it again." The mother wants to hear this from her child; the priest wants to hear this in the confessional. Jesus said, "Go, and sin no more," knowing full well that the person would no doubt sin again—but wanting that person to have the intention of not doing so.

There's no point in apologizing for a wrong-doing, then repeating the folly again and again. Contrition, confession, asking for forgiveness—saying sorry—means that you intend to stop doing what is wrong.

Parents bring up their children to know the difference between right and wrong. They teach their children to say sorry when they have done something wrong.

They teach them what the word "sorry" means.

By their own example, parents teach their children about forgiveness.

For a young child, forgiveness can mean that even though they have done something wrong, Mommy and Daddy still love them.

But a child should not grow up thinking he or she can do anything, however bad, then simply say sorry and automatically be forgiven. It can be difficult for parents to get the balance right.

Part of the parents' role is to teach their child moral values—the difference between right and wrong, that wrong is harmful, and that saying "sorry" must mean feeling sorry.

A child also needs to learn how to forgive. With siblings, school friends —even with their parents—children must learn to forgive those who have wronged them.

For young children, this is a difficult lesson to learn, because in the early years they are inherently self-centered. But as they grow, they must learn that if they expect to be forgiven, they too must forgive.

The teens are a very confusing time for many children. Intellectually, absolutes become relative; concepts like **"truth"** and **"fact"** become more malleable. Physically, their bodies explode with hormones and growth. Emotionally, feelings become incredibly intense.

Teenagers feel pain,
rejection, betrayal,
and loss of love as the
worst things in the world.

Pokkharasâdi said to the Blessed One: "He is young and foolish, Gotama, that young Brahman Ambattha. Forgive him, Gotama."

Ambattha Sutta
(Buddhist scriptures)

Teenage behavior may be troublesome and require much patience and forgiveness. But it is important for parents to remember the other side of the coin: Teenagers themselves have a lot to forgive.

Because the teens are emotionally intense as well as formative years, it is crucial that parents, relatives, and friends do everything possible to help teenagers grow through this difficult time in their lives. And this includes forgiving them, over and over again.

Intense hurts, if not dealt with, lie deeply buried—but they are not inert. Think how often a young person in their late teens or early twenties says to their mother, "I thought you didn't love me any more, after I did so-and-so."

The mother might say, "I forgave you that a long time ago."

The youngster replies, "**But I didn't know. You never told me**."

This is commonplace. Because a teenager wasn't told she was forgiven, she may have spent years feeling unloved and rejected. The scars from this can last a lifetime.

Sometimes parents are so judgmental of their "wayward" children that the possibility of forgiveness is lost altogether, and a rift develops that is never bridged. It is tragic when parents will not forgive their children for being different from them.

See the little old-world village
Where her aged parents live
Drinking the champagne she sends them
But they never can forgive

World War I song of a girl who
"lost her honest name," Anonymous

Teenagers need to learn to forgive, too.

Close friends will let them down. Boyfriends or girlfriends will betray them. Teenagers feel these emotions intensely. Learning to forgive others, and so be able to rebuild seemingly shattered friendships, is one of the most valuable lessons a teenager can learn.

Her sins, which are
many, are forgiven,
for she loved much;
but to whom little is
forgiven, the same
loveth little.

Luke 7:47

Teenagers need to forgive their parents—often a lot!

The problem with being a parent is, there are few courses. There are no practice runs. It's on-the-job training. As a parent, you learn from your mistakes. And that means that you make mistakes. Many of them are trivial, but some, for the teenager, may be hugely important.

If you explode at your teenage child for coming home late—not knowing that the bus had broken down, or that she had escorted a sick friend home—then she will understandably feel resentful.

Once you have learned the facts, you need to apologize, and give your child the opportunity to forgive you.

"Not so, thou most ungrateful unto God, thou more cruel than the lion, the tiger, and the crocodile, for even savage beasts tend their young, whilst thou didst reject thine own, because thou heldest the white hair given unto him by his Creator for a reproach in the sight of men. O faint of heart, arise and seek thy child, for surely one whom God hath blessed can never perish. And turn thou unto him and pray that he forgive thee."

The Shah Namah (The Epic of Kings) (Persian sacred text)

Children begin by loving their parents; as they grow older they judge them; rarely, if ever, do they forgive them.

Oscar Wilde (1854–1900)

Youth, which is forgiven everything,
forgives itself nothing;
Age, which forgives itself anything,
is forgiven nothing.

George Bernard Shaw (1856–1950)

Sometimes, much later in life, people realize that they are still angry—often legitimately angry—at their mother or father, for the way they were brought up, or for unfortunate and painful events that occurred during their childhood or teens.

It is important to deal with this anger, to recognize it, accept it, examine the reasons for it—and then, having done that, to let go of it and move on.

And a vital part of this is forgiving your parents, whether they are still living or not—to forgive them in your heart.

If you don't forgive your parents, you can't move on. But if you recognize their faults as human failings, and forgive them, you will be more able to see your own failings as a parent, and become a better parent yourself.

But if you don't forgive your own parents for their faults and failings, you will harbor bitterness and resentment in your heart all your life. Ask yourself this: **Will that make you a better person?**

To forgive enemies
H— does pretend,
Who never in his life
forgave a friend.

MS Notebooks, William Blake
(1757–1827)

It is easier to forgive an
enemy than a friend.

Madame Dorothée Deluzy (1747–1830)

When someone is close to you, being hurt by them can feel like a terrible betrayal, and forgiving them can be difficult.

Mending a broken friendship can be hard, but surely it is better than losing the friendship. Make the effort. Keep the friend.

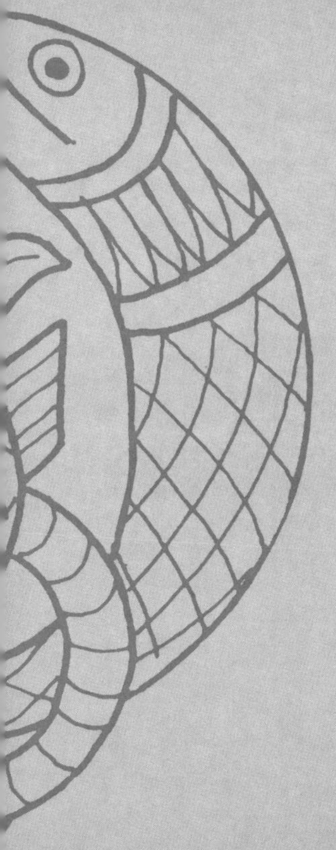

Friendships, like all relationships, take work to keep strong.

We are all human. We all make mistakes, and say or do stupid, hurtful things.

There is nothing so advantageous to a man than a forgiving disposition.

Terence (c. 185–159 B.C.E.)

May I tell you why it
seems to me a good thing
for us to remember wrong
that has been done us?
That we may forgive it.

Charles Dickens (1812–1870)

If we are not prepared to forgive our friends, we will end up having no friends.

But if we can forgive our friends their errors, we will make our friendships stronger.

What an absurd thing it is to pass over all the valuable parts of a man, and fix our attention on his infirmities.

Joseph Addison
(1672–1719)

But I say unto you which hear:
Love your enemies;
do good to them which hate you.

Luke 6:27

Forgiveness can be closely linked to love. Sometimes, forgiving someone you don't like can be the first step to liking them, and even loving them. Forgiveness means saying, "The past is gone; let's start fresh from where we are now." Forgiveness involves honesty and trust.

A fault confessed is more than half amended.

John Harington (1561–1612)

Honesty means confessing what you have done wrong—and between two people, the fault is rarely on one side alone. And so honesty also means accepting that the other person is a flawed human being, just as you are yourself.

If we had no faults, we should not take so much pleasure in remarking them in others.

François, Duc de la Rochefoucauld
(1613–1680)

Perhaps someone did something that hurt you, but if you had been them, you might have done the same—or worse. In acknowledging that, and in accepting the moral frailty of all humanity, including yourself and the person who wronged you, you have taken the first step toward forgiving them.

Forgiveness involves trust. If someone apologizes to you for hurting you, you must trust the sincerity of their apology, and their good intentions not to hurt you again. And they, in turn, are trusting you to leave their wrongdoing in the past, not to keep bringing it up as evidence of their untrustworthiness. (If you do, you have not truly forgiven them.)

If there is enough honesty and trust between two people to forgive and be forgiven, something worthwhile has been created between them—a bond, a genuine relationship.

In South Africa, after the fall of apartheid, there was debate about whether or not to set up a tribunal to punish the officials of the fallen government for violence and human rights violations. Instead, the Truth and Reconciliation Commission was set up which, instead of seeking justice (which inevitably means judgment and punishment), sought to bring out the truth as the first step to healing wounds. Those who did wrong admitted it publicly, and those who had been wronged accepted that there was nothing to be gained from holding on to old pain and old grievances, however justified.

True reconciliation does not consist in merely forgetting the past.

Nelson Mandela, 1996

The Truth and Reconciliation Commission knew that, in post-apartheid South Africa, it was time to move on, and it wasn't going to be an easy process. It still isn't for many in that troubled country who have suffered so many wrongs. But for those who are prepared to make the effort, however huge it might be, it's an important start.

. . . vengeance is not our goal. The building of a new nation at peace with itself because it is reconciled with its past, is our objective. Let us all therefore tell the truth that has to be told . . .

Nelson Mandela, 1996

Blessed are the merciful, for they shall obtain mercy.

Matthew 5:7

What doth the Lord require of thee, but to do justly, and to love mercy, and to walk humbly with thy God.

Micah 6:8

If we have sinned against the man who loves us, have ever wronged a brother, friend, or comrade, The neighbor ever with us, or a stranger, O Varuna, remove from us the trespass. If we, as gamesters cheat at play, have cheated, done wrong unwittingly or sinned of purpose, Cast all these sins away like loosened fetters, and, Varuna let us be thine own beloved.

Rig Veda (Hindu scriptures)

marriage and forgiveness

Love is the most important thing in most people's lives. A loving relationship is at the center of the home and family. Whether there are two of you or a whole tribe, it is love that binds you all together.

But love is fragile. It is easily hurt, easily damaged. Little things you would shrug off if said or done by a stranger, can, when said by your lover, fester and destroy your relationship.

No close and loving partnership is ever free of tension.

If a relationship falls apart at the first disagreement, there can't have been much to it. If two people are to live together, share their lives, their home, and their bed, they have to learn very early on the vital importance of dealing with the problems that are bound to arise between them.

In a good relationship, learning how to cope with tensions and resolve them satisfactorily helps make the relationship stronger and the love deeper.

And blessings on the falling out
That all the more endears,
When we fall out with those we love
And kiss again with tears!

Alfred, Lord Tennyson (1809–1892)

One of the most important aspects of making a relationship work is learning how to forgive. It's also vital to know how to ask for, and accept, forgiveness. And of course, you need to know when to ask for forgiveness, when to apologize.

You may think that you are fairly easy to get on with, and that your partner is the difficult one.

Think again!

Think how easy it is to say a harsh word. Think how often your partner has let you down, by forgetting about something they'd promised to do, by being late, by not supporting you when you needed it, or by being dismissive of something important to you. Think how often your partner has hurt you, in little and big things.

Now think how often you have done the same to your partner.

Do you remember all the times your partner has hurt you and store them up in a library of grievance, neatly indexed, so you can throw them at your partner the next time you have an argument and they accuse you of something?

If so, ask yourself this: Do you want your relationship to fall apart in bitterness and recrimination? (Because that is what will happen.) Or do you want to find a way to deal with these problems?

If you continually refer to old hurts, bringing them up in moments of conflict, you have not truly forgiven your partner. You must put the past behind you.

If you can't say you're sorry, and mean it, then you shouldn't be in a relationship. And if you can't excuse your partner's faults and failings, you shouldn't be in a relationship.

There are three words that are most important in maintaining a good relationship:

Not "I love you."

But "I was wrong."

Sometimes you should say you are sorry even when you know you are in the right—because your partner might know equally well that **they** are in the right. Unless at least one of you gives way, you're at an impasse, and you'll never get anywhere.

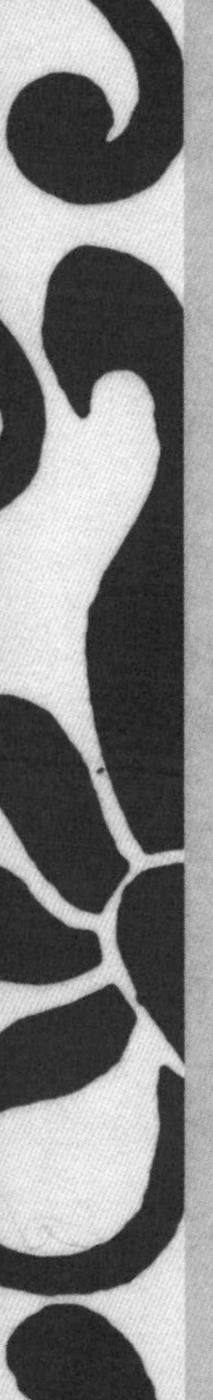

Sometimes in an argument, even when you are in the right (if it can be as simple as that), you should back down. Why? Because you love your partner, because you don't want to destroy their pride, because you don't want to hurt them any further—and because you do want your relationship to work.

If your partner is important to you, sometimes you need to swallow your own pride, and give in to them.

A soft answer turneth
away wrath;
but grievous words
stir up anger.

Proverbs 15:1

Ask yourself:

Which is more important, the toast being burned again, or our relationship? **Which is more important**, the car not being washed, or our relationship? **Which is more important**, having to wait a half-hour because my partner is late, or our relationship?

If you love your partner, none of the petty things they do that annoy you is worth losing your relationship over. Your relationship, based on love, is bigger than any of these irritations.

Life is full of petty annoyances; it's just that they seem worse when they are caused by the person closest to us. But how important are they really? Important enough to let them destroy your relationship?

Your partner keeps doing irritating, careless things—but ask yourself, "How perfect am I?" Why is it such a big thing when your partner turns up late, but an unimportant irrelevance when you do? Why should you expect them to excuse or ignore your failings, if you're going to get so irritated at theirs?

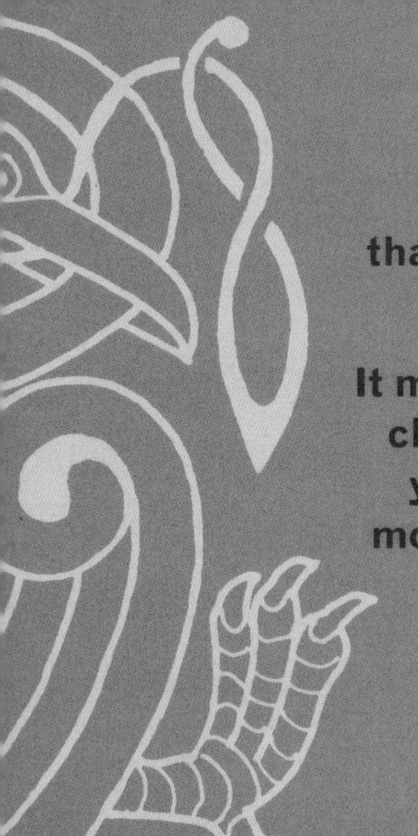

A relationship means working together, and that means giving and taking.

It means having to climb down from your position of moral superiority.

It means saying sorry.

A relationship means forgiving your partner's failings, mistakes, carelessness, and harsh words.

And it means apologizing for your own mistakes, and seeking to make amends.

One of the most destructive things is to leave an argument unfinished when you go to bed. It will still be unresolved in the morning. And if one of you stays awake half the night turning the argument over in your mind, it will be much worse by the morning. Apart from the fact that you'll be tired and irritable, you will have added to this argument all the other grievances you've been storing up.

How do you avoid this? How do you sleep well together after an argument?

When her rage is at its height, when it is open war between you, then beg her to ratify a peace upon her bed; she'll soon make friends. 'Tis there that, all unarmed, sweet concord dwells; 'tis there, the cradle of forgiveness. The doves that late were fighting, more tenderly will bill and coo; their murmurs seem to tell how true and tender is their love.

The Art of Love, Ovid (43 B.C.E.–C. C.E. 17)

The Bible contains what must be the single most important piece of advice for maintaining a good marriage:

Let not the sun go down upon your wrath.

Ephesians 4:26

What can be a greater sign of love between two people than forgiveness for "**unforgivable**" behavior?

For most people, the most devastating behavior of their partner must be sexual infidelity. It is the ultimate betrayal of the love and trust of a relationship. Unsurprisingly, it is one of the most common causes of relationship breakups and often leads to acrimonious divorce. And yet millions of couples, confronted with this crushing act of betrayal, manage to stay together. How do they do it?

With forgiveness.

There's no point trying to skate over infidelity, pretending it's not important or treating it as if it never happened. A few couples claim to have a relationship where both people agree that sex is for fun, and you can just as easily have fun with other people without it harming your union. But such relationships—if they exist at all—are rare.

For most people, their partner's sexual infidelity is utterly devastating. And many would say, when they first discover it, that it is unforgivable.

The immediate reaction is vengeance—to break something dear to them, to slash all the clothes in their wardrobe, to burn their precious CDs, to smash their car windshield with a hammer. This might make you feel better for a moment—but does it help in the long run?

It may be that vengeance is sweet, and that the gods forbade vengeance to men because they reserved for themselves so delicious and intoxicating a drink. But no one should drain the cup to the bottom. The dregs are often filthy-tasting.

The River War,
Winston Churchill (1874–1965)

Indeed, revenge is always the pleasure of a paltry, feeble, tiny mind.

Juvenal (C. C.E. 60–C. 130)

Revenge can do far more harm than good—harm to yourself, as well as to the one you feel so bitter toward.

Heat not a furnace for your foe so hot
That it do singe yourself.

Henry VIII, William Shakespeare (1564–1616)

You don't need revenge.
You need to sit down together.
You need to talk.
You need to listen.

If you are the injured person, you need to make it clear how much you have been hurt, how much you feel betrayed.

If you are the offender, you need to understand just how deeply you have wounded your partner. Only then will you have the right to even begin to apologize.

And you both need to know the difference between reasons and excuses. There can be no excuse for betraying your partner through infidelity, but there may be reasons why it happened. **Through talking and listening, you may both gain understanding of those reasons.**

From understanding, eventually, comes forgiveness.

Infidelity needn't be the end of your relationship. It doesn't have to be the unforgivable sin.

There is a way out, if both people want their lives to move on together.

If there is talking, listening, understanding, acceptance of the pain of the injured one, genuine sorrow for the pain caused, and absolute determination that it will never happen again, then forgiveness can be given and received.

Giving and receiving forgiveness with understanding and trust mends a damaged relationship, brings the couple closer, and strengthens their relationship.

Forgiving the
"**unforgivable**"
isn't easy—but
it is one of the
greatest proofs
of your love.

Love is . . .
saying, "I'm sorry.
Please forgive me."

Love is . . .
saying, "I forgive you."

Love is . . .
Accepting that you've
been forgiven.

Sometimes it can be easier to forgive the big things than the little things. But daily life in a relationship is made up of thousands of little things.

If you let the little things annoy you and mount up, they can be just as destructive as one huge, "**unforgivable**" act.

Don't let this happen.

It is the piece of grit inside the shell of the oyster that causes the pearl to grow.

Instead of letting the little things irritate you, divide you from each other, cause anger and harsh words between you (which then need to be apologized for and forgiven), learn to love your partner's idiosyncrasies!

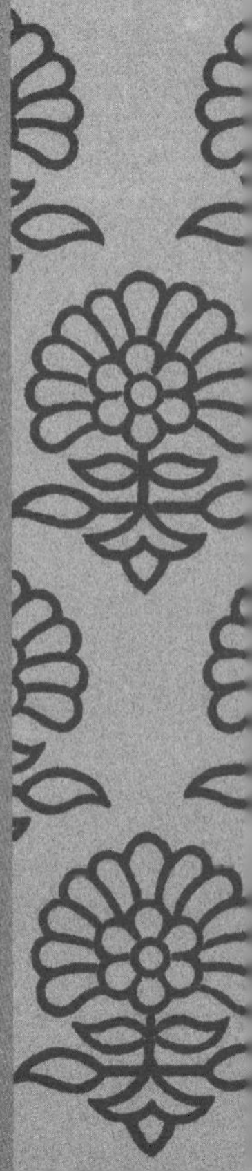

Learn to appreciate the things that make your partner different from you, that are part of their unique character.

If you see your friends' relationships in trouble because of unforgiven hurts, don't interfere—it is much better for them to work it out for themselves.

But if they confide in you, if it has reached the point where they come and tell you their problems, and ask you for advice or help, this may be because they have watched you overcome similar problems in your own relationship.

What can you tell them?

Talk. Listen.

Say sorry.

Forgive.

And accept forgiveness.

If you love your partner, forgiveness should be natural. In itself, forgiveness is an expression of love. It's proving to each other—and to the world around you—that your love is greater than all the divisive elements in life.

To say
"Of course I
forgive you"
is another
way of saying
"I love you."

Remember that you need to accept your partner's forgiveness. Don't assume it, but don't brush it off when it's given. It is important. If your partner forgives you for something you have done wrong, that is an expression of their love for you.

Accept their forgiveness with thanks. Accept their love. And grow stronger together.

The more you forgive and accept forgiveness—mutually—the more your love will grow, and be a wonder and a delight to everyone who sees you.

Forgive me, I beseech you, by the laws of our mutual love; forgive me by all the gods who lend themselves so often to thy false oaths; by that face that seems to me a thing divine, and by thine eyes which have made captives of mine. Whatever you may be, you ever will be mine. Thine it is to say whether you would have me a willing or unwilling lover. Ah, let us spread our sails and profit by the prospering gales, that, though against my will, I shall yet be forced to love.

The Love Books of Ovid (43 B.C.E.–C. C.E. 17)

Love is not love
Which alters when it alteration finds,
Or bends with the remover to remove;
O, no! it is an ever-fixed mark,
That looks on tempests and is never
  shaken

Sonnet 116, William Shakespeare (1564–1616)

looking within yourself

Forgiveness brings healing. It takes the burden of guilt from the person being forgiven, and helps them to start afresh. But it also does good to the person who is doing the forgiving.

Until you forgive someone, you have a lump of discontent within your heart that hurts you and does you harm.

Holding on to the pain that others have caused you only causes you further pain. You need to let go of it before it takes control of your whole life.

We have all met people who are so full of bitterness against others—or against the whole world—for real or imagined injustices, that they have become eaten up by their grievances, their grudges, their hatred. They turn inward, and the only thing they can focus on is their own pain—which becomes all-consuming. **It makes them tight, withered, unfriendly, unlikable.**

If you let go of old pains—your hurts, your grievances—it is like laying down a heavy burden that was bending your shoulders and crushing your spine. When you forgive someone for harm they have caused you, you are relieved of the weight of that heavy grievance. You can stand straighter, stronger, healthier.

For many people, emotional tension is felt in the belly. If someone wronged you last month, or last year, or ten years ago, and you have never forgiven them, every time you see or think of them your belly will tense and tighten. And you know that the next time you see this person—next week or next year or in ten years' time—the same thing will happen.

It is much better to deal with the problem than to fear bumping into a person you haven't forgiven and feeling emotionally tense.

It may be that this person is just as uncomfortable at seeing you. They know that they did or said something to hurt you, maybe many years ago, and that it has been left unresolved.

None of us is perfect. You may have been offended against, but do you remember how often you have offended other people?

Or do you think you are faultless?

Men's minds are too ready to excuse guilt in themselves.

Livy (59 B.C.E.–C.E. 17)

The greatest of faults is to be conscious of none.

Thomas Carlyle (1795–1881)

Have you never done wrong? Have you never caused pain to another person? Are you the only person in the world who is perfect?

Examine yourself!

Put yourself in the position of the one who has hurt you.

A long time ago you hurt someone. Whether in a large or a petty way, you did or said something that caused them pain. When you see this person today, how do you feel? Guilty? Awkward? Uncomfortable? You ask yourself: Do they remember? Do they still hurt? Are they still damaged by what you did to them?

Imagine that a person you once hurt badly comes up to you, smiles, and quietly takes you to one side. No one else is there to overhear what you both say; this is between the two of you.

It might be difficult to start off. One of you might say, "**Hey, we keep bumping into each other.**" The other might say, "**How long have we known each other now?**" It might be awkward for a little while. But if you sense that the other person is genuinely reaching out to you, and you do the same, you begin to find a place to meet.

If you rebuff someone who is willing to give you forgiveness, you are setting the old grievance in concrete; you are making it much, much worse. Do you really want to do that?

Imagine now that this person says, "You know, it took me a long time to let go of what you said to me, all those years ago. Do you remember?" And you feel deeply uncomfortable, and embarrassed, and guilty, and perhaps a little angry that the other person has brought this up. But then they say something like, "That was a long time ago, and I've been stupid to hang on to it for so long."

What do you say? Do you laugh? Do you shrug it off? Do you start finding excuses for the hurtful things you once said, justifying them?

Or do you say, "**Whatever reasons I thought I might have had at the time, I must have really hurt you when I said that. Is it too late to say 'Sorry'?**"

It is **never**
too late
to say sorry.

If the person you hurt accepts your apology and smiles and says, "**Why don't we leave that in the past, where it belongs? Life's too short to hold on to old grudges,**" then meet them in the middle.

It doesn't matter if they don't actually use the words, "**I forgive you.**"

Accept the essence of their forgiveness.

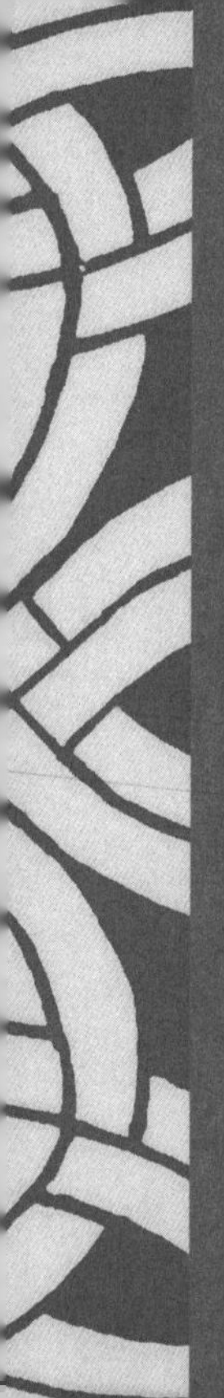

Now, how do you feel?
Relieved?
At peace?
More calm?
More relaxed?

And how do they feel?

Whichever of the two people you are in the situation just described, try to put yourself in the other person's shoes. If it was difficult for you to apologize, or to forgive, then it was just as difficult for the other person to forgive, or to apologize. Recognize the effort that the other person has made, and acknowledge it. One of you might say of the other, "That can't have been easy, after all this time."

It isn't easy to apologize, or to forgive. You need to make some movement yourself. You need to leave openings for the other person. You need to help each other, if you are to reach the goal that will heal you both. In reaching this goal, you will have created a new bond of understanding and cooperation between you.

Those who forgive most shall be most forgiven.

Philip James Bailey (1816–1902)

Forgiveness
heals.

Forgiveness
heals friendships and relationships
between people.

Forgiveness
heals the people you have forgiven.

Forgiveness
heals the person who forgives.

The quality of mercy is not strain'd
It droppeth as the gentle rain from heaven
Upon the place beneath; it is twice blest;
It blesseth him that gives and him
that takes.

Merchant of Venice, William Shakespeare (1564–1616)

No ceremony that to great ones 'longs,
Not the king's crown, nor the deputed sword,
The marshal's truncheon, nor the judge's robe,
Become them with one half so good a grace
As mercy does.

Measure for Measure, William Shakespeare (1564–1616)

When you forgive someone, you are cleansing yourself inside. You are wiping away the dark murk of resentment and bitterness that you had stored within yourself.

You are making yourself whole.

What about when someone forgives you?

Do you think, "**They don't really mean that**"? If so, you are doubting their word and their integrity. You are demeaning them.

Accept the gift of their forgiveness, and be thankful for it.

Or do you think, "**They might have forgiven me, but I can never forgive myself for what I did**"? If so, you are stopping the process of healing that began the moment they forgave you.

If you have been forgiven for something, your slate has been wiped clean—at least, on that matter. But if you won't forgive yourself, you are denying yourself healing and cleansing inside.

The most
difficult
person to
forgive is
yourself.

Forgiveness to the injured does belong;
But they ne'er pardon, who have done
the wrong

John Dryden (1631–1700)

You may pardon much to others, nothing to yourself.

Decimus Magnus Ausonius (fl. C.E. 380)

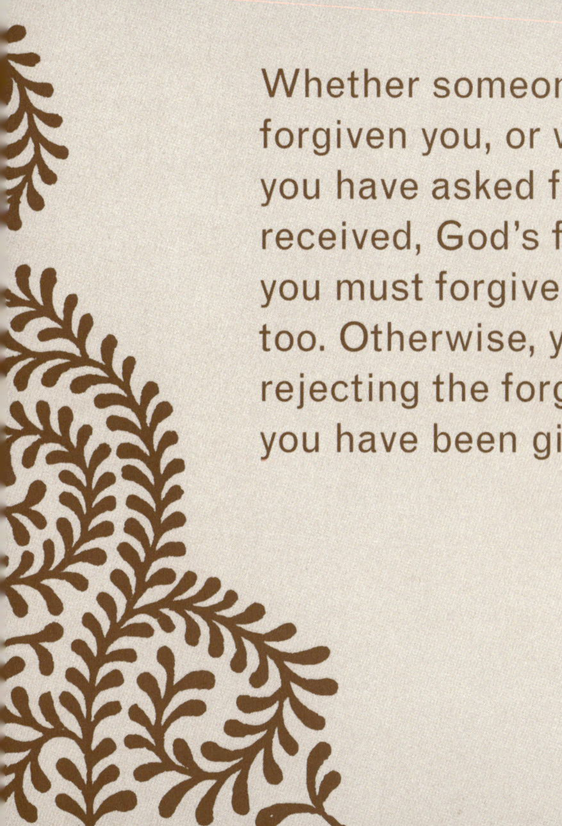

Whether someone else has forgiven you, or whether you have asked for, and received, God's forgiveness, you must forgive yourself too. Otherwise, you are rejecting the forgiveness you have been given.

A good conscience is to the soul what health is to the body; it preserves constant ease and serenity within us, and more than countervails all the calamities and afflictions which can befall us without.

Joseph Addison (1672–1719)

A guilty conscience is a terrible thing. Just like the bitterness which eats you up because you haven't forgiven someone else, if you know that you have done wrong, and have done nothing about it, the guilt will not let you rest.

A fool does not know when he commits his evil deeds: but the wicked man burns by his own deeds, as if burnt by fire.

The Dhammapada (Buddhist scriptures)

From the body of one guilty deed a thousand ghostly fears and haunting thoughts proceed.

William Wordsworth (1770–1850)

There is no witness so terrible, no accuser so powerful, as the conscience that dwells within us.

Sophocles (496–406 B.C.E.)

There is another man within me that's angry with me, rebukes, commands, and dastards me.

Sir Thomas Browne (1605–1682)

How do you deal with your own guilt?

You confess it, both to God and to the person you have hurt. And you ask for their forgiveness.

Guilt is a heavy burden to carry. Guilt can weigh you down to the ground. But asking for forgiveness lifts that burden off your shoulders, so that you can stand straight again, and face the world without self-loathing.

"Come unto me, all ye that labor and are heavy laden, and I will give you rest."

Matthew 11:28

Forgiveness brings blessings, to the forgiver and the forgiven. Open your eyes. Be ready to receive those blessings. Don't miss out on them!

The poet then passes on to the subject of the need for constant watchfulness, in order to avoid the snares of the world, and not to miss the divine blessing whenever it may appear. There is a tradition, "When half the night has passed Allah will descend to earth, and cry, 'Ho, ye that ask, it shall be answered to you; and ye that crave pardon, it shall

be pardoned to you; and ye that petition, your petitions shall be granted.'" But all who sleep the sleep of negligence will miss the promised blessing. This is illustrated by the story of a lover who obtained an assignation with his mistress, but when she came, was found asleep, and was accordingly rejected.

The Masnavi Book 6, Rumi (1207–1273) (Sufi writings)

By oneself the evil is done, by oneself one suffers; by oneself evil is left undone, by oneself one is purified. Purity and impurity belong to oneself, no one can purify another.

The Dhammapada (Buddhist scriptures)

why we need forgiveness

Let us not forget that the reason we need forgiveness from God is that we are sinners.

God is perfect;
we are not.

God is loving;
we are full of hatred.

God is peaceful;
we are full of anger
and war.

God is pure;
we are sullied.

God is selfless;
we are selfish.

Most of the world's religions teach the same message: that sin separates us from God. It is a barrier between us.

How can a perfect God want anything to do with sinful people? How can we break through this barrier that separates us from God?

God is willing to do His part to bring us back together . . .
. . . but first we must do our part.

If we want God to forgive us, first we must acknowledge our sin, confess it, and ask for forgiveness.

For thy name's sake, O Lord, pardon mine iniquity; for it is great.

Psalm 25:11

Now while these things were passing in the land of Iran, Afrasiyab wandered over the earth, and he knew neither rest nor nourishment. And his soul was unquiet, and his body was weary, and he feared danger on all sides. And he roamed till that he found a cavern in the side of a mountain, and he crept into it for rest. And he remained a while within the cave pondering his evil deeds, and his heart was filled with repentance. And he prayed aloud unto God that He would grant him forgiveness of his sins, and the cries of his sorrow rent the air.

The Shah Namah (The Epic of Kings)
(Persian sacred text)

O God, my God! Be Thou not far from me, for tribulation upon tribulation hath gathered about me.

O God, my God! Leave me not to myself, for the extreme of adversity hath come upon me.

Out of the pure milk, drawn from the breasts of Thy loving-kindness, give me to drink, for my thirst hath utterly consumed me.

Beneath the shadow of the wings of Thy mercy shelter me, for all mine adversaries with one consent have fallen upon me.

Keep me near to the throne of Thy majesty, face to face with the revelation of the signs of Thy glory, for wretchedness hath grievously touched me.

With the fruits of the Tree of Thine Eternity nourish me, for uttermost weakness hath overtaken me.

From the cups of joy, proffered by the hands of Thy tender mercies, feed me, for manifold sorrows have laid mighty hold upon me.

With the broidered robe of Thine omnipotent sovereignty attire me, for poverty hath altogether despoiled me.

Lulled by the cooing of the Dove of Thine Eternity, suffer me to sleep, for woes at their blackest have befallen me.

Before the throne of Thy oneness, amid the blaze of the beauty of Thy countenance, cause me to abide, for fear and trembling have violently crushed me.

Beneath the ocean of Thy forgiveness, faced with the restlessness of the leviathan of glory, immerse me, for my sins have utterly doomed me.

Prayers and Meditations by Bahá'u'lláh
(Bahá'í scriptures)

Do not hurl at us thy club, thy divine bolt; be not incensed at us, O lord of cattle! Shake over some other than us the celestial branch!

Injure us not, interpose for us, spare us, be not angry with us! Let us not contend with thee!

Hymns of the Artharva-Veda (Hindu scriptures)

Therefore I make these
penances, Supreme
Comfort me, who am Thine,
and terrified;
Forgive me, for I would be
innocent;
Have pity, Lord of lords! on me
and these.

The Mahabharata (Hindu scriptures)

If we confess our sins, he is faithful and just to forgive us our sins, and to cleanse us from all unrighteousness.

If we say that we have not sinned, we make him a liar, and his word is not in us.

1 John 1:9–10

I beg of Thee, O my Best Beloved, to pardon me and those who earnestly seek to promote Thy Cause; Thou art indeed the One Who forgiveth the sins of all mankind.

Selections from the Writings of the Báb (Bahá'í scriptures)

I acknowledged my sin unto thee, and mine iniquity have I not hid. I said, I will confess my transgressions unto the Lord; and thou forgavest the iniquity of my sin.

Psalm 32:5

God our Lord! Protect us through Thy grace from whatsoever may be repugnant unto Thee and vouchsafe unto us that which well beseemeth Thee. Give us more out of Thy bounty and bless us. Pardon us for the things we have done and wash away our sins and forgive us with Thy gracious forgiveness. Verily Thou art the Most Exalted, the Self-Subsisting.

Selections from the Writings of the Báb (Bahá'í scriptures)

Almighty and most merciful Father, We have erred and strayed from thy ways like lost sheep. We have followed too much the devices and desires of our own hearts. We have offended against thy holy laws. We have left undone those things which we ought to have done, And we have done those things which we ought not to have done, And there is no health in us.

But thou, Oh Lord, have mercy upon us, miserable offenders. Spare thou them, O God, which confess their faults. Restore thou them that are penitent, According to thy promises declared unto mankind in Christ Jesus our Lord.

And grant, O most merciful Father, for his sake, That we may hereafter live a godly, righteous, and sober life, To the glory of thy holy name.

Book of Common Prayer

The ignorant clown will never understand.
Again and again, he becomes engrossed
in entanglements.
He listens to the sounds of sin and the
music of corruption, and he is pleased.
His mind is too lazy to listen to the
Praises of the Lord.
You do not see with your eyes—you are
so blind!
You shall have to leave all these
false affairs.
Says Nanak, please forgive me, God.

Shri Guru Granth Sahib: Raag Soohee
(Sikh scriptures)

Although we be unworthy, through our manifold sins, to offer unto thee any sacrifice, yet we beseech thee to accept this our bounden duty and service; not weighing our merits, but pardoning our offences.

Book of Common Prayer

Wilt thou forgive that sin, where I begun,
Which is my sin, though it were done before?
Wilt thou forgive those sins through which I run
And do them still, though still I do deplore?
When thou hast done, thou hast not done,
  For I have more.

Wilt thou forgive that sin, by which I have won
Others to sin, and made my sin their door?
Wilt thou forgive that sin which I did shun
A year or two, but wallowed in a score?
When thou hast done, thou hast not done,
  For I have more.

Hymn to God the Father, John Donne (c. 1572–1631)

Be thou patient, then; verily, God's promise is true: and ask thou forgiveness for thy sins, and celebrate the praise of thy Lord in the evening and in the morn.

The Koran 40:55 (Islamic scripture)

He's half absolv'd
who has confess'd.

Matthew Prior (1664–1721)

Sin is not just wrong actions, but also wrong words, and even wrong thoughts.

How can mere words and thoughts be sins? Words can be weapons; think how hurtful an unkind word can be. We probably do more harm with our careless words than we do with our actions.

Verily I say, the tongue is for mentioning what is good, defile it not with unseemly talk. God hath forgiven what is past. Henceforward everyone should utter that which is meet and seemly, and should refrain from slander, abuse, and whatever causeth sadness in men.

Kitáb-i-Aqdas (Bahá'í scriptures)

As for thoughts, the thought gives birth to the act. If we start to think of people with anger and hatred, it will not be long before we display this in our actions toward them.

And as for "sins of the flesh," the Bible tells us that if a man looks on a woman with lust, he has already committed adultery with her in his heart.

Our sinful thoughts may be hidden deep inside us, but they can do great harm.

They can eat us up from the inside.

A heart full of bitterness,
anger, and revenge may not always
show on our faces—smiles can
be false—but it will surely
show in our lives.

However secret
our sinful thoughts might be,
they do harm to others,
and they separate us
from God.

God can see into our hearts.

However good we might appear in the sight of others, if our hearts are black, God sees it, and sorrows.

Repent therefore of
this thy wickedness, and
pray God, if perhaps the
thought of thine heart
may be forgiven thee.

Acts 8:22

Then hear thou from heaven thy dwelling place, and forgive, and render unto every man according unto all his ways, whose heart thou knowest; (for thou only knowest the hearts of the children of men).

2 Chronicles 6:30

Who can tell how oft he offendeth:
O cleanse thou me from my secret faults.

Keep thy servant also from presumptuous sins, lest they get the dominion over me: so shall I be undefiled, and innocent from the great offence.

Let the words of my mouth, and the meditation of my heart, be always acceptable in thy sight, O Lord my strength and my redeemer.

Psalm 19:12–14, *Book of Common Prayer*

Our sin is in our hearts, in the judgements we make of other people's actions when we ourselves are impure, and in not letting go of these destructive thoughts once they have arisen.

A young monk who had just taken his vows went off to the mountains to meditate, with an elderly monk to teach him. They came to a fast-flowing stream, and on its bank was a woman, frightened to cross. The elderly monk picked up the woman and carried her across, and set her down; she thanked him, and went on her way. The young monk was scandalized.

"**Our vows forbid us ever to touch a woman!**" he cried. "**How could you do this?**" "**I have set her down**," said the elderly monk, "**but you are still carrying her.**"

Whether it is our actions, our words, or our deeds, sin is harmful to us— and to others.

We may think that if we do something wrong, and get away with it, then we have done no harm. But who knows what harm we may have done to others? There might be consequences we do not know of, a cascade of harm we had never intended.

Our sins have consequences.

Sometimes others, and God, may forgive us for our sins, but the harm that we have done cannot be reversed.

Sometimes the innocent suffer because of our sins; and even though we have been forgiven, the innocent still suffer.

In the *Old Testament* book of *Samuel* there is a well known cautionary tale. King David commits adultery with Bathsheba and gets her pregnant, then sends her husband Uriah to his certain death in battle. The prophet Nathan helps David to realize his wickedness, and David begs God for forgiveness. But the innocent child, the product of his sin, is born sickly, and, despite David's heartfelt prayers, dies a week later.

Sin harms ourselves, but also causes great pain and suffering to others, including the most innocent of people. And saying sorry does not always put that right.

But sin does its greatest harm deep inside our own hearts. We may not see it, but it is working away within us, eating at us from the inside.

When the Bible says, "Be sure your sin will find you out," it is not just talking about being caught for doing wrong. It is talking about our inner sin eating away at us until it becomes obvious outside us.

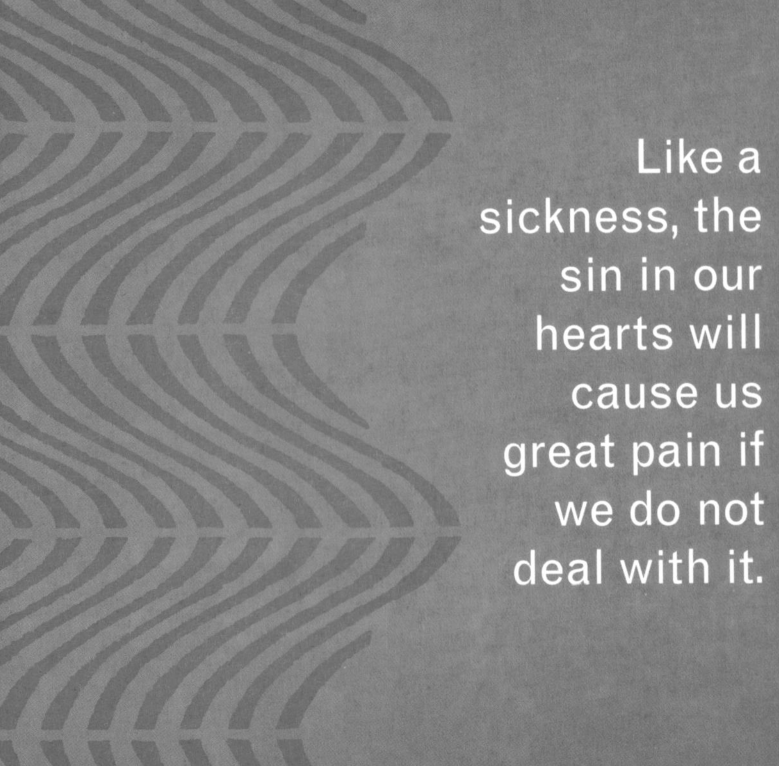
Like a sickness, the sin in our hearts will cause us great pain if we do not deal with it.

Asking for God's forgiveness takes away even this deep, inner poison, and makes us clean inside.

Our sin brings guilt, which can be just as destructive as sin itself. Guilt burdens us with feelings of uncleanliness, unworthiness, and sorrow. These feelings themselves cause us great harm.

Once God has forgiven our sin, we should let the guilt go. If we have been forgiven, our hearts are made clean.

Look upon mine affliction and my pain; and forgive all my sins.

Psalm 25:18

I am but a poor creature, O my Lord; I have clung to the hem of Thy riches.

I am sore sick; I have held fast the cord of Thy healing.

Deliver me from the ills that have encircled me, and wash me thoroughly with the waters of Thy graciousness and mercy, and attire me with the raiment of wholesomeness, through Thy forgiveness and bounty.

Fix, then, mine eyes upon Thee, and rid me of all attachment to aught else except Thyself.

Aid me to do what Thou desirest, and to fulfill what Thou pleasest.

Prayers and Meditations by Bahá'u'lláh
(Bahá'í scriptures)

So that contrariwise ye ought rather to forgive him, and comfort him, lest perhaps such a one should be swallowed up with overmuch sorrow.

2 Corinthians 2:7

O Nanak, wicked are the uncountable actions of the mind.

They bring terrible and painful retributions, but if the Lord forgives me, then I will be spared this punishment.

Shri Guru Granth Sahib: Raag Soohee
(Sikh scriptures)

And the prayer of faith shall save the sick, and the Lord shall raise him up; and if he have committed sins, they shall be forgiven him.

Confess your faults one to another, and pray one for another, that ye may be healed. The effectual fervent prayer of a righteous man availeth much.

James 5:15–16

She is sick, O my God, and hath entered beneath the shadow of the Tree of Thy healing; afflicted, and hath fled to the City of Thy protection; diseased, and hath sought the Fountain-Head of Thy favors; sorely vexed, and hath hasted to attain the Well-Spring of Thy tranquillity; burdened with sin, and hath set her face toward the court of Thy forgiveness.

Attire her, by Thy sovereignty and Thy loving-kindness, O my God and my Beloved, with the raiment of Thy balm and Thy healing, and make her quaff of the cup of Thy mercy and Thy favors. Protect her, moreover, from every affliction and ailment, from all pain and sickness, and from whatsoever may be abhorrent unto Thee.

Thou, in truth, art immensely exalted above all else except Thyself. Thou art, verily, the Healer, the All-Sufficing, the Preserver, the Ever-Forgiving, the Most Merciful.

Prayers and Meditations by Bahá'u'lláh
(Bahá'í scriptures)

Let a wise man blow off the impurities of his self, as a smith blows off the impurities of silver one by one, little by little, and from time to time.

The Dhammapada
(Buddhist scriptures)

the *joy* of God's forgiveness

When we hear preachers thundering about our sins and iniquities, and how our hearts are as black as coal, we can easily forget the joy there is in God's forgiveness.

We forget that forgiveness is a positive thing.

The point of confessing our failings to God is not to make us feel bad about ourselves, but to open us up to the joy of receiving God's forgiveness.

With the joy of God's forgiveness comes freedom, peace, oneness with God, and fellowship and closeness with other people.

Forgiveness is God's way of accepting us back into the divine presence.

For any believer, this is the greatest blessing, knowing that we are welcomed by God.

Bless the Lord, O my soul, and forget not all his benefits:

Who forgiveth all thine iniquities; who healeth all thy diseases;

Who redeemeth thy life from destruction; who crowneth thee with loving kindness and tender mercies;

Who satisfieth thy mouth with good things; so that thy youth is renewed like the eagle's.

Psalm 103:2–5

Whatever betide us, we beseech Thine ancient forgiveness, and seek Thine all-pervasive grace. Our hope is that Thou wilt deny no one Thy grace, and wilt deprive no soul of the ornament of fairness and justice.

Prayers and Meditations by Bahá'u'lláh
(Bahá'í scriptures)

Blessed is he whose transgression is forgiven, whose sin is covered.

Blessed is the man unto whom the Lord imputeth not iniquity, and in whose spirit there is no guile.

Psalm 32:1–2

Forgiveness brings blessings

and joy

and warmth

and love

and strength

and protection

with the arms of God around us.

One who belongs to the All-powerful Lord and
Master—no one can destroy him.
The Lord's servant remains under His protection;
The Lord Himself forgives him, and blesses him
with glorious greatness.
There is none higher than Him.
Why should he be afraid? What should he
ever fear?

Through the Guru's Teachings, peace and
tranquillity abide within the body.
Remember the Word of the Shabad, and you
shall never suffer pain.
You shall not have to come or go, or suffer
in sorrow.
Imbued with the Naam, the Name of the Lord,
you shall merge in celestial peace.
O Nanak, the Gurmukh beholds Him ever-
present, close at hand.
My God is always fully pervading everywhere.

Shri Guru Granth Sahib: Raag Soohee
(Sikh scriptures)

Sin is a barrier between ourselves and God. It separates us from God. But if we ask for forgiveness, and accept His forgiveness, that barrier is torn down.

I have blotted out, as a thick cloud, thy transgressions, and, as a cloud, thy sins: return unto me; for I have redeemed thee.

Sing, O ye heavens; for the Lord hath done it: shout, ye lower parts of the earth: break forth into singing, ye mountains, O forest, and every tree therein: for the Lord hath redeemed Jacob, and glorified himself in Israel.

Isaiah 44:22–23

Forgiveness demonstrates to us the greatness of God.

If God is perfect and pure, He must be disgusted by our sins and failings. And yet in His love He forgives us.

This is a God whose greatness cannot be imagined! This is a God so great He is willing to forgive us!

The scriptures of all the world's religions rejoice in the greatness of God, as shown by God's willingness to forgive us and welcome us back into divine company.

When we confess our sins, and receive God's forgiveness, and accept that we are truly forgiven, then we can know ourselves in the presence of God.

Grant, O my Lord, that they who have ascended unto Thee may repair unto Him Who is the most exalted Companion, and abide beneath the shadow of the Tabernacle of Thy majesty and the Sanctuary of Thy glory. Sprinkle, O my Lord, upon them from the ocean of Thy forgiveness what will make them worthy to abide, so long as Thine own sovereignty endureth, within Thy most exalted kingdom and Thine all-highest dominion. Potent art Thou to do what pleaseth Thee.

Prayers and Meditations by Bahá'u'lláh
(Bahá'í scriptures)

Look not on my state, O my God, nor my failure to serve Thee, nay rather regard the oceans of Thy mercy and favors, and the things that beseem Thy glory and Thy forgiveness and befit Thy loving-kindness and bounties. Thou art, verily, the Ever-Forgiving, the Most Generous.

Prayers and Meditations by Bahá'u'll'áh
(Bahá'í scriptures)

For thou, Lord, art good, and ready to forgive; and plenteous in mercy unto all them that call upon thee.

Psalm 86:5

I implore Thee, O my Lord, by Thine Ark, through which the potency of Thy will was manifested and the energizing influences of Thy purpose were revealed, and which saileth on both land and sea through the power of Thy might, not to seize me in my mighty sins and great trespasses. I swear by Thy glory! The waters of Thy forgiveness and Thy mercy have emboldened me, as hath Thy dealing, in bygone ages, with the sincere among Thy chosen ones, and with such of Thy Messengers as have proclaimed Thy oneness.

Prayers and Meditations by Bahá'u'lláh
(Bahá'í scriptures)

If someone slanders the True Guru, and then comes seeking the Guru's Protection, the True Guru forgives him for his past sins, and unites him with the Saints' Congregation.

When the rain falls, the water in the streams, rivers, and ponds flows into the Ganges; flowing into the Ganges, it is made sacred and pure.

Such is the glorious greatness of the True Guru, who has no vengeance; meeting with Him, thirst and hunger are quenched, and instantly, one attains celestial peace.

O Nanak, behold this wonder of the Lord, my True King! Everyone is pleased with one who obeys and believes in the True Guru.

Shri Guru Granth Sahib: Raag Bilaaval (Sikh scriptures)

O children of men! If ye believe in the one True God, follow Me, this Most Great Remembrance of God sent forth by your Lord, that He may graciously forgive you your sins. Verily He is forgiving and compassionate toward the concourse of the faithful.

Selections from the Writings of the Báb
(Bahá'í scriptures)

Even if the Guru rebukes me, He still seems very sweet to me. And if He actually forgives me, that is the Guru's greatness.

Shri Guru Granth Sahib: Raag Soohee
(Sikh scriptures)

I beseech Thee, however, O Thou Who art the Enlightener of the world and the Lord of the nations, at this very moment when, with the hands of hope, I have clung to the hem of the raiment of Thy mercy and Thy bounty, to forgive Thy servants who have soared in the atmosphere of Thy nearness, and set their faces toward the splendors of the light of Thy countenance, and turned unto the horizon of Thy good pleasure, and approached the ocean of Thy mercy, and all their lives long have spoken forth Thy praise, and have been inflamed with the fire of their love for Thee. Do Thou ordain for them, O Lord my God, both before and after their death, what becometh the loftiness of Thy bounty and the excellence of Thy loving-kindness.

Prayers and Meditations by Bahá'u'lláh (Bahá'í scriptures)

He who created the Universe, gives sustenance to it.

The One Lord alone is the Great Giver.
He Himself is the True Master.

That True Lord is always with you; the Gurmukh is blessed with His Glance of Grace.

He Himself shall forgive you, and merge you into Himself; forever cherish and contemplate God.

The mind is impure; only the True Lord is pure.
So how can it merge into Him?

God merges it into Himself, and then it remains merged; through the Word of His Shabad, the ego is burnt away.

Shri Guru Granth Sahib: Raag Soohee
(Sikh scriptures)

There is, verily, no God but Him, the Mighty, the Well-Beloved. Glorified art Thou, O Lord, Thou forgivest at all times the sins of such among Thy servants as implore Thy pardon. Wash away my sins and the sins of those who seek Thy forgiveness at dawn, who pray to Thee in the day-time and in the night season, who yearn after naught save God, who offer up whatsoever God hath graciously bestowed upon them, who celebrate Thy praise at morn and eventide, and who are not remiss in their duties.

Selections from the Writings of the Báb
(Bahá'í scriptures)

O Thou in separation from Whom hearts and souls have melted, and by the fire of Whose love the whole world hath been set aflame! I implore Thee by Thy Name through which Thou hast subdued the whole creation, not to withhold from me that which is with Thee, O Thou Who rulest over all men!

Thou seest, O my Lord, this stranger hastening to his most exalted home beneath the canopy of Thy majesty and within the precincts of Thy mercy; and this transgressor seeking the ocean of Thy forgiveness; and this lowly one the court of Thy glory; and this poor creature the orient of Thy wealth. Thine is the authority to command whatsoever Thou willest. I bear witness that Thou art to be praised in Thy doings, and to be obeyed in Thy behests, and to remain unconstrained in Thy bidding.

Kitáb-i-Aqdas (Bahá'í scriptures)

Who is a God like unto thee, that pardoneth iniquity, and passeth by the transgression of the remnant of his heritage? He retaineth not his anger for ever, because he delighteth in mercy.

He will turn again, he will have compassion upon us; he will subdue our iniquities; and thou wilt cast all their sins into the depths of the sea.

Micah 7:18–19

Praised be Thou, O Lord my God! The tongues of all created things testify to Thy sovereignty and Thine omnipotence, and proclaim mine own poverty and my wretchedness when face to face with the revelations of Thy wealth. Look, then, O my God, upon this sinner whose gaze hath, at all times, been fixed upon the source of Thy forgiveness, and whose eyes have been bent upon the horizon of Thy grace and Thy gifts.

Prayers and Meditations by Bahá'u'lláh
(Bahá'í scriptures)

Forgiveness
is the key to
the doorway
to a new life.

When you accept the key of God's forgiveness, you can step through the door into the presence of God.

Everything
changes.

On a human level, forgiveness helps to close gaps, build bridges.

When you forgive someone, you feel peace, a new cleanness within yourself. And so do they.

When you are forgiven by someone, you feel peace, a new cleanness, within yourself. And so do they.

If forgiveness is mutual, it is an act of cooperation between two people. And working together, they come closer together.

So imagine how it is with God.

When you feel cut off from God because of your wrong thoughts, words, or deeds, asking for and receiving forgiveness enables you to feel God's closeness again.

Instead of feeling estranged from God because of your sin, you can open the door onto the divine presence, and feel God's perfection washing over you.

Forgiveness,
whether you give it or are given it,
brings peace, joy, liberation,
a new life.

**This is why forgiveness
is such a blessing.**

Because forgiveness,
given and accepted,
takes away the knot
of guilt inside us and
cleans away the poison
of self-hatred that
unforgiven sin leaves
in our heart, we emerge
stronger and healthier,
not just in spirit and
mind, but in body also.

The fever and sickness are gone, and the diseases are all dispelled.

The Supreme Lord God has forgiven you, so enjoy the happiness of the Saints.

All joys have entered your world, and your mind and body are free of disease.

So chant continuously the Glorious Praises of the Lord; this is the only potent medicine.

So come, and dwell in your home and native land; this is such a blessed and auspicious occasion.

O Nanak, God is totally pleased with you; your time of separation has come to an end.

Sri Guru Granth Sahib: Raag Soohee
(Sikh scriptures)

I am a sinner, O my Lord, and Thou art the Ever-Forgiving.

As soon as I recognized Thee, I hastened to attain the exalted court of Thy loving-kindness.

Forgive me, O my Lord, my sins which have hindered me from walking in the ways of Thy good-pleasure, and from attaining the shores of the ocean of Thy oneness.

Prayers and Meditations by Bahá'u'lláh
(Bahá'í scriptures)

Repent ye therefore, and be converted, that your sins may be blotted out, when the times of refreshing shall come from the presence of the Lord.

Acts 3:19

As to those who truly believe in God and are well assured in the signs revealed by Him, perchance He will graciously forgive them the things their hands have committed, and will grant them admission into the precincts of His mercy. He, in truth, is the Ever-Forgiving, the Compassionate.

Selections from the Writings of the Báb
(Bahá'í scriptures)

Come now, and let us reason together, saith the Lord: though your sins be as scarlet, they shall be as white as snow; though they be red like crimson, they shall be as wool.

If ye be willing and obedient, ye shall eat the good of the land:

But if ye refuse and rebel, ye shall be devoured with the sword: for the mouth of the Lord hath spoken it.

Isaiah 1:18–20

Bless them, O my God, and ascribe unto them such glory as hath shone forth above the horizon of Thy will, and hath shed its splendors from the kingdom of Thine utterance. Immerse them, O my Lord, beneath the ocean of Thy mercy, and illumine them with the dawning light of Thy Revelation.

Forgive, then, O my God, their fathers and their mothers, by Thy favour, and Thy bounty, and Thy tender mercies. Send, then, upon them from the right hand of Thy most exalted Paradise the fragrance of the robe of Thine all-glorious Beauty. Potent art Thou to do what pleaseth Thee. Thou, verily, art the Governor, the Ordainer, the All-Bountiful, the Ever-Forgiving, the Most Generous.

Selections from the Writings of the Báb
(Bahá'í scriptures)

For thou, Lord, art good, and ready to forgive; and plenteous in mercy unto all them that call upon thee.

Give ear, O Lord, unto my prayer; and attend to the voice of my supplications.

In the day of my trouble I will call upon thee: for thou wilt answer me.

Psalm 86:5–7

I yield Thee such thanks as can cause Thee to forgive all sins and trespasses, and to fulfill the needs of the peoples of all religions, and to waft the fragrances of pardon over the entire creation.

I yield Thee such thanks as can enable them that recognize Thy unity to scale the heights of Thy love, and cause such as are devoted to Thee to ascend unto the Paradise of Thy presence.

Selections from the Writings of the Báb
(Bahá'í scriptures)

For thy name's sake, O Lord, pardon mine iniquity; for it is great.

What man is he that feareth the Lord? him shall he teach in the way that he shall choose.

His soul shall dwell at ease; and his seed shall inherit the earth.

The secret of the Lord is with them that fear him; and he will shew them his covenant.

Psalm 25:11–14

Let us go, O my companions, and understand our God; with the spell of virtue, let us obtain our Lord God.

He is called the Lover of His devotees; let us follow in the footsteps of those who seek God's Sanctuary.

If the soul-bride adorns herself with compassion and forgiveness, God is pleased, and her mind is illumined with the lamp of the Guru's wisdom.

With happiness and ecstasy, my God enjoys her; I offer each and every bit of my soul to Him.

Shri Guru Granth Sahib: Raag Soohee
(Sikh scriptures)

And I will cleanse them from all their iniquity, whereby they have sinned against me; and I will pardon all their iniquities, whereby they have sinned, and whereby they have transgressed against me.

And it shall be to me a name of joy, a praise and an honor before all the nations of the Earth, which shall hear all the good that I do unto them: and they shall fear and tremble for all the goodness and for all the prosperity that I procure unto it.

Jeremiah 33:8–9

Mercy may prevail over vengeance, and give
the hypocrite
Such light as is not possessed by the full moon.
God may purge his dealings from that hypocrisy,
And in mercy wash him clean of that defilement.
In order that the pardoning grace of God may
be seen,
God pardons all sins that need pardon.

The Masnavi Book 5, Rumi (1207–1273) (Sufi writings)

Almighty God, our heavenly Father, who of his great mercy hath promised forgiveness of sins to all them that with hearty repentance and true faith turn unto him; Have mercy upon you, pardon and deliver you from all your sins; confirm and strengthen you in all goodness; and bring you to everlasting life.

Book of Common Prayer

For so the holy sages once
did sing
That He our deadly forfeit
should release,
And with His Father work
us a perpetual peace.

John Milton (1608–1674)

For the reward of virtue and the forgiveness of sins, I do deeds of righteousness for the love of my soul. May all virtuousness of all good ones of the Earth of seven climes reach the width of the Earth, the length of the rivers, the height of the sun in their original form. May it be righteous, live long. Thus may it come as I wish.

The Zend Avesta: Khorda Avesta
(Zoroastrian scriptures)

Thy loving providence hath encompassed all created things in the heavens and on the Earth, and Thy forgiveness hath surpassed the whole creation. Thine is sovereignty; in Thy hand are the Kingdoms of Creation and Revelation; in Thy right hand Thou holdest all created things and within Thy grasp are the assigned measures of forgiveness.

Thou forgivest whomsoever among Thy servants Thou pleasest.

Verily Thou art the Ever-Forgiving, the All-Loving. Nothing whatsoever escapeth Thy knowledge, and naught is there which is hidden from Thee.

Selections from the Writings of the Báb
(Bahá'í scriptures)

How do we receive this bounty from God? By confessing our faults, by asking for His forgiveness, and by accepting His forgiveness.

And then God will make us whole, and let us rest in His presence.

Chasing with light our sin away, O Agni, shine
thou wealth on us.
May his light chase our sin away.
For goodly fields, for pleasant homes, for
wealth we sacrifice to thee.
May his light chase our sin away.
Best praiser of all these be he; foremost, our
chiefs who sacrifice.
May his light chase our sin away.
So that thy worshippers and we, thine, Agni,
in our sons may live.
May his light chase our sin away.
As ever-conquering Agni's beams of splendor
go to every side,
May his light chase our sin away.

Rig Veda (Hindu scriptures)

making it right

Just saying sorry
is not enough.
We need to mean it.

We need contrition
and confession.

But then we need to do
something.

We need to follow on from
the word sorry.

Every mother teaches her naughty child that he must mean "sorry," not just say it. The priest in the confessional will say the same: If you are really sorry, if you really want forgiveness, then you must be determined not to do this again.

True repentance means changing your life. Jesus said, "Go, and sin no more." That may not be possible, because as humans we are weak and selfish at heart—but at least we should try.

If we ask our mother, our lover, a priest, or God, to forgive us for something we have done wrong, while having every intention of doing it again as soon as we can, is that genuine repentance?

If the forgiveness we ask for is supposed to heal us, how can it possibly do so unless we are determined to turn away from that particular sin?

The best way to turn away from doing wrong is to turn toward doing good.

We need to turn our lives around.

Let the wicked forsake his way, and the unrighteous man his thoughts: and let him return unto the Lord, and he will have mercy upon him; and to our God, for he will abundantly pardon.

Isaiah 55:7

If my people, which
are called by my
name, shall humble
themselves, and pray,
and seek my face, and
turn from their wicked
ways; then will I hear
from heaven, and will
forgive their sin, and
will heal their land.

2 Chronicles 7:14

O Lord, open thou my lips
And my mouth shall show forth thy praise
For thou desirest not sacrifice, else would I give it;
    Thou delightest not in burnt offering.
The sacrifices of God are a broken spirit;
A broken and a contrite heart, O God
Thou wilt not despise.

Psalm 51:15–17

God is like a loving parent.

God can be imagined in many ways—as Shepherd, Judge, Guide, Comforter, or as loving Parent.

Though in many traditions people think of God as being a Father, it is just as valid to think of Her as our Mother.

Both fathers and mothers love their children, raise them, teach them, care for them—and over and over and over again, forgive them. In this way, as in so many others, God is our loving, caring, forgiving parent.

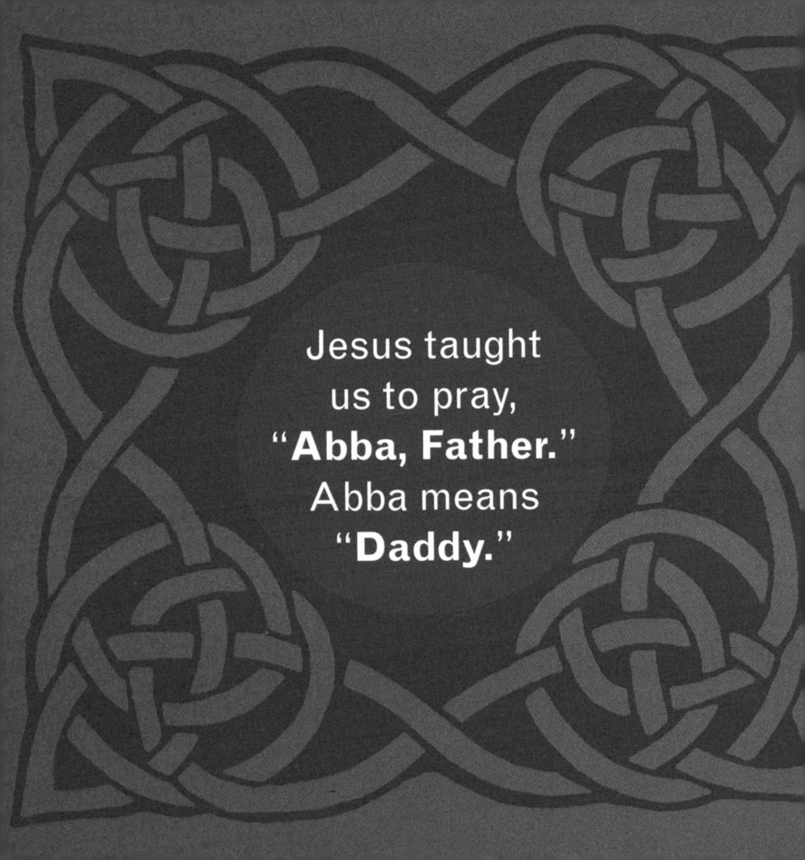

Jesus taught
us to pray,
"**Abba, Father.**"
Abba means
"**Daddy.**"

When we ask God for forgiveness, we are like a small child saying sorry to our Mommy or Daddy—and just as we knew that because Mommy or Daddy loved us, they would forgive us, so it is with God.

If we confess to God, and mean it, we can have absolute trust that we will be forgiven.

And the son said unto him, Father, I have sinned against heaven, and in thy sight, and am no more worthy to be called thy son.

But the father said to his servants, Bring forth the best robe, and put it on him; and put a ring on his hand, and shoes on his feet:

And bring hither the fatted calf, and kill it; and let us eat, and be merry:

For this my son was dead, and is alive again; he was lost, and is found. And they began to be merry.

Luke 15:21–24

But thou art a God
ready to pardon,
gracious and merciful,
slow to anger, and of
great kindness, and
forsookest them not.

Nehemiah 9:17

To the Lord our God belong
mercies and forgivenesses,
though we have rebelled
against him.

Daniel 9:9

As far as the east is from the west, so far hath he removed our transgressions from us.

Like as a father pitieth his children, so the Lord pitieth them that fear him.

For he knoweth our frame; he remembereth that we are dust.

As for man, his days are as grass: as a flower of the field, so he flourisheth.

For the wind passeth over it, and it is gone; and the place thereof shall know it no more.

But the mercy of the Lord is from everlasting to everlasting upon them that fear him, and his righteousness unto children's children;

To such as keep his covenant, and to those that remember his commandments to do them.

Psalm 103:12–18

We must learn to forgive.

If we hope to be forgiven for our own faults—by God or by other people—we have to be prepared to forgive. If we harbor resentment and bitterness toward someone for something they have done to us, how can we possibly ask for, or expect, forgiveness for our own misdeeds?

If we forgive others, they are more prepared to forgive us. If we don't, what right do we have to ask them to forgive us?

Anyone who asks for forgiveness has to be prepared to give it.

Forgiving other people for the hurt they have done to us helps to bring peace, both within ourselves, and between ourselves and those we have forgiven.

Forgiving others can have another remarkable effect.

It can be an example to others.

All of us harbor grudges, complaints against others, and bitterness for old wrongs—whether real or imagined.

If I see someone being forgiving to a person who has hurt them, that will cause me to look within myself, and see what old pains I am holding on to. Then I can let go of them, by forgiving the person who hurt me. Then I too can be an exemplar of forgiveness, for others to follow.

And forgive us our sins; for we also forgive every one that is indebted to us. And lead us not into temptation; but deliver us from evil.

Luke 11:4

Him I call indeed a Brahmana who is tolerant with the intolerant, mild with fault-finders, and free from passion among the passionate. Him I call indeed a Brahmana from whom anger and hatred, pride and envy have dropt like a mustard seed from the point of a needle. Him I call indeed a Brahmana who utters true speech, instructive and free from harshness, so that he offend no one.

The Dhammapada (Buddhist scriptures)

And when ye stand praying, forgive, if ye have ought against any: that your Father also which is in heaven may forgive you your trespasses.

But if ye do not forgive, neither will your Father which is in heaven forgive your trespasses.

Mark 11:25–26

Brothers in humanity
who live after us, let
not your hearts be
hardened against us,
for, if you take pity on
us poor ones, God
will be more likely to
have mercy on you.
But pray God that he
may be willing to
absolve us all.

François Villon (1431–c. 1463)

Take heed to yourselves:
If thy brother trespass
against thee, rebuke him;
and if he repent, forgive him.

Luke 17:3

Then came Peter to him, and said, Lord, how oft shall my brother sin against me, and I forgive him? till seven times?

Jesus saith unto him, I say not unto thee, Until seven times: but, Until seventy times seven.

Matthew 18:21–22

We must learn
the importance of
making things right
with others.

Forgiving others means talking with them first.

Too many friendships break up, too many relationships are irreparably soured—and on a larger scale, too many wars begin—because we stop talking to each other.

Sometimes this can be difficult, if the pain is old, and deep-seated.

But if you're not prepared to talk, you can't apologize, you can't ask for forgiveness, and you can't grant forgiveness.

For as long as there is silence between you, there is a wall that nothing can break through—certainly not forgiveness.

But if you talk—and listen—and together seek to find a way through the pain, then the wall is broken down, and forgiveness brings peace.

Opening up the communication between two parties is the first step toward forgiveness, reconciliation, and peace.

Remember that as you forgive your brother, your lover, or your friend, at the same time they may be forgiving you.

Harboring a grudge and not forgiving someone harms them—and also harms you, because you are carrying that bitterness within you. Forgiveness heals you both.

Forgiveness must be mutual; otherwise the pain continues.

When you have told someone you forgive them, ask them if there is any way you have hurt them that you might not be aware of. And if there is, ask them to forgive you.

That way, you will clear the air between you and throw away all the harmful resentments that slowly poison you from the inside. You can start afresh, closer than before.

And you can learn to forgive yourself.

If the person you have hurt
has forgiven you,

and if God
has forgiven you,

then you must also
forgive yourself.

If you don't forgive yourself, you are throwing back the forgiveness you have been given into the face of the person who forgave you—and you are putting yourself above God.

If God can forgive you, you have no right not to forgive yourself.

And all is past, the sin is sinned, and I,
Lo! I forgive thee, as Eternal God
Forgives: do thou for thine own soul
the rest.

Idylls of the King, Alfred, Lord Tennyson (1809–1892)

There was a certain creditor which had two debtors; the one owed five hundred pence, and the other fifty.

And when they had nothing to pay, he frankly forgave them both. Tell me therefore, which of them will love him most?

Simon answered and said, I suppose that he, to whom he forgave most. And he said unto him, Thou hast rightly judged.

Luke 7:41–43

And if he trespass against thee seven times in a day, and seven times in a day turn again to thee, saying, I repent; thou shalt forgive him.

Luke 17:4

Joy go with thee and her, happily joined.
But say, Nishadha, wrought I any jot
Wrongful to thee, whilst sojourning unknown
Within my walls? If any word or deed,
Purposed or purposeless, hath vexed thee, friend,
For one and all thy pardon grant to me!

The Mahabharata (Hindu scriptures)

And above all things have fervent charity among yourselves: for charity shall cover the multitude of sins.

I Peter 4:8

And be ye kind one to another, tenderhearted, forgiving one another, even as God for Christ's sake hath forgiven you.

Ephesians 4:32

If, during the Paggusan, among monks or nuns occurs a quarrel or dispute or dissension, the young monk should ask forgiveness of the superior, and the superior of the young monk. They should forgive and ask forgiveness, appease and be appeased, and converse without restraint. For him who is appeased, there will be success (in control); for him who is not appeased, there will be no success; therefore one should appease one's self.

The Kalpa Sutra of Bhadrabahu. Life of Mahavira
(Jain scriptures)

Moreover if thy brother shall trespass against thee, go and tell him his fault between thee and him alone: if he shall hear thee, thou hast gained thy brother.

But if he will not hear thee, then take with thee one or two more, that in the mouth of two or three witnesses every word may be established.

Matthew 18:15–16

O careless straggler, bind a rope upon thy feet,
Lest thou lose even thine own self!
But thy ingratitude and unthankfulness
Forget the honey draft thou hast sipped.
That road was perforce closed to thee
When thou didst wound the hearts of the men
of heart.
Quick! clasp them and ask pardon of them;
Like the clouds, shed tears of lamentation,
So that their rose-garden may bloom for thee,
And their ripe fruits burst open of themselves.

The Masnavi Book 3, Rumi (1207–1273)
(Sufi writings)

And forgive thy people that have sinned against thee, and all their transgressions wherein they have transgressed against thee, and give them compassion before them who carried them captive, that they may have compassion on them.

I Kings 8:50

Judge not, and ye shall not be judged: condemn not, and ye shall not be condemned: forgive, and ye shall be forgiven:

Give, and it shall be given unto you; good measure, pressed down, and shaken together, and running over, shall men give into your bosom. For with the same measure that ye mete withal it shall be measured to you again.

Luke 6:37–38

And blessed be the King, who hath forgiven
My wickedness to him, and left me hope
That in mine own heart I can live down sin
And be his mate hereafter in the heavens
Before high God.

Idylls of the King, Alfred, Lord Tennyson (1809–1892)

the difficulties of forgiveness

Forgiveness is not always easy. But why should it be? Someone has wronged us; we have been hurt. To forgive them takes an effort.

If forgiveness were easy,
there would be no virtue in it.

Forgiveness is a virtue.

It is an act of love, kindness,
reconciliation, and often,
of sacrifice.

Forgiveness is giving—giving
something of ourselves
to someone else.

There are some things that seem too difficult to forgive. In *Marriage and Forgiveness* we looked at adultery, the ultimate betrayal in a loving relationship between two people—and at how even that can be forgiven.

There are other acts that might seem to be unforgivable: murder, rape, child abuse, and war crimes.

For many people, these acts would seem too big to be forgiven. How can you forgive something as dreadful as murder? But to think such atrocities cannot be forgiven is to misunderstand forgiveness.

Forgiveness is not saying
that a terrible act is all right
or acceptable or that
it doesn't really matter.
If a woman forgives the man
who murdered her husband,
she is not saying that it was
all right for him to murder
her husband. If it were,
she would have no
need to forgive him!

Forgiving someone for an act is not the same as condoning the act.

Listen to the victims of terrorist acts in the United States, in the Middle East, and elsewhere.

One bereaved person says, astonishingly, "I forgive those who murdered my daughter."

Another says, "Those who murdered my daughter are evil scum who must not be allowed to live. I shall not rest until all Catholics [or Protestants, or Jews, or Muslims] are destroyed."

Which person will bring peace to the world?

Which one will have peace in their heart?

The fault of others is easily perceived,
but that of one's self is difficult to perceive;
a man winnows his neighbor's faults like
chaff, but his own fault he hides, as a cheat
hides the bad die from the gambler.

The Dhammapada
(Buddhist scriptures)

The person who stores up hatred and bitterness, revenge and retribution—however terrible the crime or atrocity which causes them to do so—ultimately becomes no different from those who committed the original act. To want to see a criminal punished is an understandable human reaction. But in the end, is it the best reaction for creating peace?

Forgiveness can be the beginning of bringing an end to murder, rape, and war.

Forgiveness is healing.

Forgiveness can bring peace.

At the start of the twenty-first century, compare South Africa and Zimbabwe. The former is a country that is actively working for peace and reconciliation. In the latter country, people will not forgive the past, and acts of violence continue to plague the country.

Which is the better way?

The way of forgiveness.

Mutual Forgiveness of each vice
Such are the Gates of Paradise

William Blake (1757–1827)

Is there a line that can be drawn between those sins that are forgivable, and those that are not?

Rabbis, priests, and imams face this question every day. Moral theologians struggle with it.

**There is no easy answer.
To try to give one would be folly.**

Whatever the answer, somewhere within it will be contrition, and forgiveness.

If Jesus could say of his killers—

Father, forgive them, for they know not what they do.

Luke 23:34

—surely we should strive to do the same.

To err is human,
to forgive, divine.

Alexander Pope (1688–1744)

If God, who is perfect, can forgive people for their sins, surely we must do the same. We must not say:

> God may pardon you,
> but I never can.

Elizabeth I (1533–1603)
to the Countess of Nottingham

Neither should we say:

You ought certainly to forgive them as a Christian, but never to admit them in your sight, or allow their names to be mentioned in your hearing.

Mr. Collins in *Pride and Prejudice*,
Jane Austen (1775–1817)

This is not forgiveness;
this is hypocrisy.

We know that God, who is perfect, will forgive our sins if we genuinely repent of them, confess them, and ask His forgiveness. In all religions, God has promised us this. It is God's divine guarantee:

Confess, and your sins will be forgiven.

O thou eternally just and good,
O source of happiness,
incline thine ear unto me
and listen to my voice.
If I have sinned, if I have strayed in the
paths of Ahriman, behold my
repentance and pardon me.

The Shah Namah (The Epic of Kings)
(Persian sacred text)

'Verily, O king, it was sin that overcame you in acting thus. But inasmuch as you look upon it as sin, and confess it according to what is right, we accept your confession as to that. For that, O king, is custom in the discipline of the noble ones, that whosoever looks upon his fault as a fault, and rightfully confesses it, shall attain to self-restraint in future.'

Samanna-Phala Sutta (Buddhist scriptures)

But we should not be complacent about receiving God's forgiveness ourselves, as some have been:

I shall be an autocrat: that's my trade.
And the good Lord will forgive me:
that's his.

Catherine the Great (1729–1796)

God will pardon me,
it is His trade.

Heinrich Heine (1797–1856),
on his deathbed

To take God's forgiveness for granted
is to make God our servant.

Just because you know God will
forgive you does not mean that you
can do whatever you like,
then ask his forgiveness,
and get away with it.

Yes, God will wipe your slate clean of sins. Yes, being a fallible human, you will add to that slate again, and it will need to be wiped clean again, and God will do so. But you should not deliberately sin, in the knowledge that you will be forgiven.

Remember that forgiveness depends on:

Confession—acknowledging that you have sinned;
Contrition—being genuinely sorry for it;
Determination—not to go out and repeat that sin;
Accepting the forgiveness.

If you confess a particular sin, with the full expectation that you will go on committing it again and again, what is your confession worth?

Nothing.

You can often fool
other people.

You can sometimes fool
yourself.

But you can never fool God.

God knows what is in your heart.

He knows if your confession is genuine.

If after confessing your sin, you don't feel fully absolved, ask yourself:

How genuine was my confession?

If your confession was false, deep down inside you will know that. You will know that you didn't really mean it.

And so in your heart, soul, and spirit,
you know that you cannot accept the
forgiveness that is offered to you.
You know that to do so would be a lie.

But if your confession is genuine,
you know, deep inside, that you are forgiven.

The peace and joy of knowing this are incomparable.

Sometimes it is more difficult to forgive those we are close to. But it is vital that we do so.

We read that we ought to forgive our enemies; but we do not read that we ought to forgive our friends.

Cosimo de' Medici (1389–1464)

It is important to remember that we are all human, and we are all fallible. We all make mistakes. We all lose our tempers. We all do selfish things.

If I do these things, I should not be surprised that you do.

And so we need to seek to understand each other.

If someone does something wrong, we need to ask why. Usually there is a reason. And if we can learn the reason, we reach a greater understanding of the person who has wronged us.

To understand all
is to forgive all.

Mme. de Staël (1766–1817)

Know all
and you will pardon all.

Thomas à Kempis (c. 1380–1471)

This is not to whitewash other people's bad behavior. Wrong is wrong, whatever the reason.

A reason is not the same as an excuse.

But it can help lead to understanding, and to forgiveness.

If the injured one
could read your heart,
you may be sure
he would understand
and pardon.

Robert Louis Stevenson (1850–1894)

Understanding the reasons for bad behavior is helpful, but the main prerequisite for forgiveness must be the regret and apology of the person who has done the wrong.

We should not be profligate in our forgiveness, handing out absolution like a pack of candy.

He who forgives readily only invites offence.

Pierre Corneille (1606–1684)

Pray you now,
forget and forgive.

King Lear, William Shakespeare
(1564–1616)

We are told we should forgive and forget. This means that we should not keep raking up past wrongs, once they have been confessed and forgiven.

Forgive the sinner,
not the sin.

But in order to learn from experience, we should not forget the harmful act itself.

The stupid neither forgive nor forget; the naïve forgive and forget; the wise forgive but do not forget.

Thomas Szasz, 1973

Yet "forgive and forget" remains a good general guideline, if difficult to follow.

We are not saints. We might not be able to forget the offending actions or words—but if we can manage to forget our offense at them, that is a good start.

We should also be wary of those who offer us shallow friendship, who hope to win favor with us by false praise. Sometimes, it seems, their very presence demands forgiveness!

The man that hails you Tom or Jack,
And proves by thumps upon your back
   How he esteems your merit,
Is such a friend, that one had need
Be very much his friend indeed
   To pardon or to bear it.

William Cowper (1731–1800)

Human nature is strange. Often it is difficult to forgive ourselves, even though others have forgiven us for the harm that we have done to them.

But also, perversely, we sometimes feel resentful to the people we have harmed, as if it is their fault: Feeling guilty at what we have done to them, we make them the cause of our guilt, and blame them.

It is often easier to forgive those who have wronged us than those whom we have wronged.

Oscar Hammling (b. 1890)

Some, indeed, blame God for our faults, or at least for making us so that we are likely to commit those faults.

Oh Thou, who Man of baser Earth didst make,
And who with Eden didst devise the Snake;
For all the Sin wherewith the Face of Man
Is blackened, Man's Forgiveness give—and take!

The Rubaiyat of Omar Khayyam

Reason to rule, but
mercy to forgive:
The first is law, the last
prerogative

The Hind and the Panther, John Dryden
(1631–1700)

Humans are not machines. Humans have the capacity to forgive. Machines do not—they have no mercy.

People can be merciful.
And whichever religion you follow,
you know that God is merciful—
indeed, the font of all mercy.

If we follow God's way, we shall know divine mercy.

The Venerable Ascetic Mahavira's parents were worshippers of Parsva and followers of the Sramanas. During many years they were followers of the Sramanas, and for the sake of protecting the six classes of lives they observed, blamed, repented, confessed, and did penance according to their sins. On a bed of Kusa-grass they rejected all food, and their bodies dried up by the last mortification of the flesh, which is to end in death. Thus they died in the proper month, and, leaving their bodies, were born as gods in Adbhuta Kalpa. Thence descending after the termination of their allotted length of life, they will, in Mahavideha, with their departing breath, reach absolute perfection, wisdom, liberation, final Nirvana, and the end of all misery.

Akaranga Sutra (Jain scripture)

. . . have ye looked
At Edyrn? have ye seen how nobly changed?
This work of his is great and wonderful.
His very face with change of heart is changed.
The world will not believe a man repents:
And this wise world of ours is mainly right.
Full seldom doth a man repent, or use
Both grace and will to pick the vicious quitch
Of blood and custom wholly out of him,
And make all clean, and plant himself afresh.
Edyrn has done it, weeding all his heart
As I will weed this land before I go.
I, therefore, made him of our Table Round,
Not rashly, but have proved him everyway
One of our noblest, our most valorous,
Sanest and most obedient . . .

Idylls of the King, Alfred, Lord Tennyson (1809–1892)

Surely goodness and mercy shall follow
me all the days of my life;
And I will dwell in the house of the Lord
for ever.

Psalm 23:6

Acknowledgments

Extracts from the Authorized Version of the bible (The King James Bible), the rights in which are vested in the Crown, are reproduced by permission of the Crown's Patentee, Cambridge University Press.

Extracts from The Book of Common Prayer, the rights of which are vested in the Crown, are reproduced by permission of the Crown's Patentee, Cambridge University Press.

Extracts from Shri Guru Granth Sahib: Raag Bilaaval, and Shri Guru Granth Sahib: Raag Soohee reproduced by permission of Sign Sahib Sant Singh Khalsa.

Page 72 (bottom). Quotation used by permission of the Society of Authors, on behalf of the Estate of George Bernard Shaw.

Many thanks to the Baha'i Publishing Trust, UK, for their assistance.

Note: Every effort has been made to trace and contact copyright holders; the publisher would be pleased to hear from any copyright holders not acknowledged.

JAY VICKERS

Jay Vickers has been a teacher of religious studies and English, a computer programmer and intelligence analyst for the British and American governments, and a journalist. Vickers has been a full-time freelance writer since 1991, researching and writing mainly on religious and esoteric subjects. Currently researching for a Ph.D. in sociology of religion at the University of London, Jay is a frequent speaker on this subject at conferences and on radio and television.

Under other names, Vickers's many books include major studies of new religious movements, and a historical analysis of the beliefs of secret societies.

A regular book critic for numerous newspapers, magazines, and websites, Jay Vickers lives in London, England.

Published by MQ Publications Limited
12 The Ivories, 6–8 Northampton Street, London N1 2HY
Tel: 020 7359 2244   Fax: 020 7359 1616

Senior editor: Salima Hirani
Design: Bet Ayer

ISBN: 1–84072–400–5

Printed and bound in China